I0560001

TRIBULATION AS WRATH

RETHINKING THE TIMING OF GOD'S JUDGMENT

L. J. ANDERSON

LAMAD PRESS

Copyright © 2025 by L. J. Anderson

www.ljandersonbooks.com

Published by Lamad Press, PO Box 50477, Billings MT, 59105, www.lamad press.com

ISBN 978-1-963291-13-1 (paperback) and 978-1-963291-14-8 (ebook)

All rights reserved.

No portion of this book may be reproduced in any form without written permission from the publisher or author, except as permitted by US copyright law.

Unless otherwise noted, Scripture quotations are from the ESV® Bible (The Holy Bible, English Standard Version®), © 2001 by Crossway, a publishing ministry of Good News Publishers. Used by permission. All rights reserved.

Book cover by Jenn Anderson

First edition 2025

CONTENTS

Dedication   1

Abstract   2

Preface   3

1. Introduction   7

2. Scriptures Regarding Divine Wrath in Revela-   10
    tion

3. The Prewrath and Posttribulation Views on   13
    Divine Wrath in Revelation

4. Counterarguments to the Prewrath and Post-   20
    tribulation Views

5. The Value of Acknowledging the Possibility of   31
    a Later Outpouring of Wrath

6. So What?   34

7. Conclusion   36

A Brief Call to Action   39

Also by L. J. Anderson   40

Bibliography   41

About the author   43

To those who still tremble at the Word of God:
May you never downplay his wrath,
forget his justice,
or lose sight of the urgency of his return.
Stand firm. Speak boldly. The Lamb is coming.

ABSTRACT

Tribulation as Wrath offers a focused examination of the theme of divine wrath in the book of Revelation, arguing that the entire Tribulation, beginning with the seal judgments, is an expression of God's wrath. In doing so, it challenges the central assumptions of prewrath and midtribulational rapture views, which attempt to delay divine wrath to later judgments. Through close exegetical analysis of key texts (including Revelation 6, 14, and 15–16), the book contends that Scripture presents God's wrath as present from the outset, not merely culminating in the bowl judgments. While remaining pastorally sensitive and open to refinement, the book defends a modified pretribulational framework and calls the church to take seriously the implications of divine judgment. Evangelistic urgency, personal holiness, and doctrinal clarity are not secondary concerns, they are necessary responses to a vision of God's wrath that is both imminent and righteous. This work serves as a foundational piece in a broader eschatological project and is intended for scholars, pastors, and serious readers seeking a biblically grounded, theologically responsible understanding of end-times judgment.

PREFACE

The book you are reading is the result of scholarly research presented in a format accessible to the general public. Normally, a work like this would not be published in this form. It would almost certainly appear as a journal article—technically accessible, but realistically out of reach for most Christians. This is simply because very few Christians who haven't attended Bible college read academic journal articles in their pursuit of God. However, many do read books.

Even pastors often find it difficult to engage with journal articles regularly, though they may have a large collection of books. Presenting research in book form, similar in depth and length to a journal article, means it can potentially reach a much broader audience. That is why virtually all of my journal-length writings are, or will be, published as short books. My goal is to provide solid academic research without requiring readers to locate or gain access to academic journals.

Additionally, I hope more authors and scholars will join me in this endeavor. Independent publishing offers many benefits and only a few significant drawbacks, namely, the lack of peer review and brand recognition. Authors who are not yet widely known often depend on the credibility of the publisher's name. Peer review, for its part, plays an important role in academic publishing, acting as a gatekeeper to prevent poor scholarship from reaching publication. Where possible, I welcome peer-reviewed engagement with these ideas in journal articles, responses, and academic dialogue.

However, peer review does not guarantee high-quality work, just as the absence of peer review does not necessarily imply poor quality. In many ways, true peer review begins after publication, when the broader academic community has the opportunity to evaluate and respond to the work. In this model, peer engagement happens post-publication, as scholars interact with the material in print, online forums, public reviews, and future publications.

While still largely untested, this publishing model shows promise as an alternative method of making academic research accessible. The majority of scholars continue to view independent publishing as significantly inferior to peer-reviewed articles or works released by traditional academic presses.

The following note expands on the mission behind Lamad Press and my broader goals as an independent scholar-publisher.

Theological Publishing with Purpose

L. J. Anderson is pioneering a new approach to theological scholarship, one that is academically rigorous, biblically faithful, and institutionally independent.

Through Lamad Press, he is constructing a publishing model that restores Scripture as the primary authority in theological method while engaging seriously with the philosophical and historical challenges of Christian doctrine. His work seeks not merely to critique existing systems but to build constructive theological models that speak to the most enduring tensions in Christian thought.

At the heart of this mission is Anderson's development of Structural Theism, a theological framework that accounts for the internal identity of God by emphasizing divine structure over classical simplicity. Structural Theism affirms the reality of Trinitarian distinction, upholds the relational depth of God revealed in Scripture, and seeks to avoid the conceptual pitfalls of both eternal generation and impersonal metaphysics. It is a model designed to preserve God's oneness and threeness without collapsing into modalism, metaphysical abstraction, or tritheism.

One key expression of this model is the Incarnational Monogenetic Model, which offers a biblically grounded alternative to the doctrine of eternal generation by locating the Son's identity not in timeless derivation, but in his incarnational role and mission as uniquely begotten of the Father.

Though dealing with a different doctrinal locus,

Tribulation as Wrath reflects this same hermeneutical and theological method. Like Anderson's doctrinal models, this eschatological work emphasizes fidelity to what Scripture actually says, prioritizing literary and canonical context over inherited frameworks. By reexamining what truly constitutes God's wrath in Revelation, this book continues the broader structural theism project of questioning traditional assumptions and, if necessary, offering biblically grounded, coherent alternatives.

Unlike traditional academic pathways bound by institutional gatekeeping and publishing delays, Anderson's independent model allows for timely, coherent, and accessible scholarship, published through Lamad Press and distributed by Lamad Christian Books. His aim is to demonstrate that it is possible to do theology that is both deeply scholarly and uncompromisingly biblical, outside the confines of conventional academic systems.

Rooted in Tradition

Independent theological publishing is not a modern innovation; rather, it is a return to Christian tradition. From the Church Fathers to the Reformers, many of the most influential theologians operated outside formal institutions, writing and distributing works grounded in theological conviction, fidelity to Scripture, and service to the church. Lamad Press stands in that same stream, reviving a historic model for a new generation of biblical theology.

CHAPTER ONE

INTRODUCTION

E SCHATOLOGY IS OFTEN DISMISSED as speculative or divisive, but the question of what constitutes divine wrath in Revelation is neither. It is a question that directly impacts how one interprets the purpose of the Tribulation, the urgency of the rapture, and the nature of God's justice. If wrath begins at the very outset, as Revelation strongly suggests, then those who minimize the early judgments risk dulling the church's readiness and compromising the urgency of evangelism. This study is not about forecasting timelines or crafting sensational charts, it is about rightly understanding the Word of God and preparing the people of God to endure faithfully, proclaim boldly, and hope confidently in the Lamb who will return in judgment and glory.

A Brief History of the Debate and Its Importance

For many years after John Nelson Darby (1800-1882) first

popularized the pretribulation rapture, the rapture debate remained solely between pretribulation and posttribulation views. However, in 1941, Norman B. Harrison published *The End: Rethinking the Revelation* which is the first example of the midtribulation rapture view. Fast forward another fifty years to 1990 and Marvin J. Rosenthal published *The Prewrath Rapture of the Church*. This view predated this book somewhat as it is not only the brainchild of Rosenthal. Nevertheless, Rosenthal's book is the first full publication of the view. That said, though the prewrath view is essentially a nuanced form of the midtribulation view, both views hold that the wrath of God is not poured out until some point *later* in the Tribulation than the starting point. As such, they are both distinct from a pre or posttribulation view. The pretribulation view has held that *all* of the Tribulation entails God's wrath and thus Christians *cannot* be in the Tribulation while the posttribulation view argues that God's wrath *is* poured out in the Tribulation, but it is only on nonbelievers.

The importance of what constitutes divine wrath in eschatology likely cannot be overstated. Bart D. Ehrman writes, "The overwhelming emphasis of Revelation is not about hope but about the wrath and vengeance of God against those who have incurred his displeasure."[1] Though Ehrman is a rather liberal theologian who would not lay claim to the title "Christian," he is mostly right here. Most

---

1. Bart D. Ehrman, *Armageddon: What the Bible Really Says About the End* (New York: Simon & Schuster, 2023), XIX.

of the world is destined for the wrath and vengeance that makes up a good portion of Revelation. What constitutes divine wrath in Revelation is thus an extremely important topic as Scripture directly states that believers are *not* destined for wrath. One's view on wrath in Revelation is likely to be a major factor in one's view of the rapture. Though this book has significant ramifications on which view of the rapture is most likely, it is *not* focused on answering the rapture question. Instead, this book dives into a specific portion of eschatology that should be used to inform one's view of the rapture and the Tribulation as a whole. It addresses various arguments from multiple sides of the debate and looks at what Scripture says regarding the topic. Additionally, it engages with the benefit of acknowledging the *possibility* of a later outpouring of wrath and the ramifications that entails. This book seeks to demonstrate that the entire Tribulation involves God's wrath, but acknowledging the possibility of a later outpouring of divine wrath benefits the church and the individual.

CHAPTER TWO

SCRIPTURES REGARDING DIVINE WRATH IN REVELATION

T HE FIRST, AND ARGUABLY most important, part of this whole topic is figuring out what verses teach about God's wrath in Revelation. Some of these verses should obviously come from Revelation itself; however, because much of the Bible deals with the end times, there are other passages that need to be addressed on this topic.

Verses Outside of Revelation[1]

Romans 2:5 says, "But because of your hard and impenitent heart you are storing up wrath for yourself on the day of wrath when God's righteous judgment will be revealed." This "day of wrath" is connected to wrath, fury, tribula-

---

1. Due to length constraints, this section will be rather brief and *will not* engage with every possible reference to God's wrath in the end times. However, I plan to publish a later monograph that digs into this nuanced pretribulation view where I will engage much more heavily with these passages.

tion, and distress in Romans 2:8–9. An interesting thing to note on this passage is that the people being talked to are almost certainly believers.

First Thessalonians 1:10 says, "And to wait for his Son from heaven, whom he raised from the dead, Jesus who delivers us from the wrath to come." This passage very clearly talks about how those who "wait for his Son from heaven" will be delivered from the wrath that is to come by this very Son, Jesus. Not only is this a passage that talks about deliverance from wrath, but it is also a rapture passage as it specifically says that Christians will be "delivered...from" the wrath to come.

First Thessalonians 5:9 says, "For God has not destined us for wrath, but to obtain salvation through our Lord Jesus Christ." This is yet another verse that states that believers will not be subject to God's wrath in any way. It is arguably the most classic verse on this topic. Taking this passage more broadly also elucidates another important factor of the rapture specifically, which can impact this discussion. John Walvoord notes, "First Thessalonians 5 states that people will be saying 'peace and safety' before the great tribulation begins. This is in harmony with pretribulationism, but quite out of harmony with posttribulationalism."[2] It is also out of harmony with the prewrath view as will be seen below though Walvoord does not engage with this view at all.

---

2. Roy B. Zuck, *Vital Prophetic Issues: Examining Promises and Problems in Eschatology* (Grand Rapids, MI: Kregel, 1995), 219.

Verses in Revelation

Again, for the sake of space, not all references to *wrath* in Revelation will be addressed. There are eight distinct uses of the word; however, for the purposes of this book, the two outlined below will be sufficient.

Revelation 6:16–17 says, "'Fall on us [calling on mountains and rocks] and hide us from the face of him who is seated on the throne, and from the wrath of the Lamb, for the great day of their wrath has come, and who can stand?'" The wrath of God has come upon the world and everyone on earth hides from it seeking death as opposed to facing it. Charles Ryrie makes a good observation of the beginning of the seals being broken. He says, "The first seal is opened by the Lamb, and the wrath of what one normally considers a docile being begins to be revealed."[3] This was regarding the first seal; however, now the sixth seal has been broken and all are fully aware that the wrath of God has come.

Revelation 16:1 says, "Then I heard a loud voice from the temple telling the seven angels, 'Go and pour out on the earth the seven bowls of the wrath of God.'" These bowls are specifically designated as the "seven bowls of God's wrath." They are to be poured out on the entire earth by seven angels who are commanded by God.[4]

---

3. Charles C. Ryrie, *Revelation* (Chicago, IL: Moody Publishers, 2018), 55.

4. Grant Osborne, *Revelation* (Grand Rapids, IL: Baker Publishing, 2002), 732.

CHAPTER THREE

THE PREWRATH AND POSTTRIBULATION VIEWS ON DIVINE WRATH IN REVELATION

S INCE THE PREWRATH VIEW is essentially a nuanced view of midtribulationalism, it will be dealt with as being in one accord. The biggest difference between the views deals with the specific timing of the rapture which is beyond the scope of this book. Additionally, midtribulationism holds that the rapture happens in the midst of the Tribulation while many prewrath theologians would argue that the Tribulation and the Day of the Lord are separate events.[1] That said, if the prewrath arguments fail to satisfactorily argue for a later outpouring of wrath, then the midtribulation ones do as well. This is simply because both arguments are based on some or all of the Tribulation *not* being part of God's wrath. If it can be demonstrated

---

1. Samuel Gray Ramsey, "The Day of the Lord Separates Tribulation from Wrath" (2023). *Doctoral Dissertations and Projects*. 4760, 17. https://digitalcommons.liberty.edu/doctoral/4760 .

that *all* of the Tribulation involves God's wrath, then both views fail. Before making this attempt, it is important to see their arguments.

God's Wrath Is Only on Unbelievers

The idea that God's wrath is only on unbelievers forms the basis of the argument that posttribulationalists give. Millard Erikson writes, "According to posttribulationism, the church will be present during and experience the great tribulation."[2] The difference lies in what they argue the *source* of the wrath in the Tribulation is. God's wrath will indeed come against the world, but the Tribulation only involves Satan, the Antichrist, and wicked people's wrath against the saints.[3]

God's Wrath Is on the Day of the Lord

Among midtribulationists and prewrath rapturists, it is commonly held that the Day of the Lord constitutes God's wrath and that this Day will not involve the church. This position is also shared by most pretribulational interpreters, and even posttribulationalists often agree that the church is absent from the actual outpouring of divine wrath.

---

2. Millard Erikson, *Christian Theology* (Grand Rapids, MI: Baker Academic, 2013), 1120.

3. Ibid.

Norman B. Harrison, often regarded as the originator of the midtribulation view, argued that the Day of the Lord is directed specifically toward Israel and the nations, not the church. Drawing from Old Testament passages, he wrote,

> It [the Day of the Lord] has mainly to do with Israel's future; therefore 'that day' is called 'the time of Jacob's trouble' (Jeremiah 30:7); though it is also called 'the time of the nations' (Ezekiel 30:3). While it is thus referred to these two divisions of the race as its participants, *be it noted that it is never called the time of the Church's trouble* (emphasis added).[4]

Harrison emphasized that the church is entirely absent from the events associated with this period. The central point of disagreement among rapture views, then, is not whether the church will experience God's wrath, but how one defines the timing and scope of the Day of the Lord.

---

4. Norman B. Harrison, *The End: Re-Thinking the Revelation* (Minneapolis, MN: The Harrison Service, 1948), 18-19.

Revelation Does Not Use "Wrath" for Most/All of the Tribulation

Marvin Rosenthal writes,

> "The wrath of God is a major topic in the book of Revelation. No less than eight times the word *wrath* is used. The first occasions are in Revelation 6:16–17 in anticipation of the opening of the seventh seal. It is significant to note that not once is the word *wrath* used before Revelation 6:16–17 or in describing the six seals."[5]

The basic idea is that since the word *wrath* is not used, it is not in view here. This is one of the main arguments for the prewrath view. It is an interesting take as there are many examples in Scripture where a specific word is not used yet theologians hold to said word anyway.

This leads to their view of the rapture since the lack of the word *wrath* then suggests that the church might still be here. Thus, the rapture is likely to happen between the sixth and seventh seals. Alan Hultberg writes, "The process of opening the seals is halted in Revelation 7 in order to allow for the protection of God's servants before God's Wrath

---

5. Marvin Rosenthal, *The Pre-Wrath Rapture of the Church* (Nashville, TN: Thomas Nelson, 1990), 171.

is poured out (Rev. 7:1–3)."[6] This, consequently, is when Hultberg argues for the rapture at this point of Revelation. In his eyes, this reconciles Matthew 24 with Revelation 6 and 7.

A distinct challenge with the view that the word *wrath* is not used to describe the first five or six seals is brought up by Renald Showers when he writes,

> The Pre-Wrath argument that because the word *wrath* does not appear in the book of Revelation until after the sixth seal has been opened that no wrath of God will be administered during the Great Tribulation is a two-edged sword. If the absence of the word prompts the conclusion that no wrath of God will be administered during the Great Tribulation, then it could also prompt the conclusion that no wrath of man will be administered during the Great Tribulation.[7]

The wrath of man is another way that the prewrath argument deals with what is going on in Revelation before *wrath* is mentioned. But, as Showers states, this is just as problematic as the pretribulation view.

---

6. Alan Hultberg, *Three Views on the Rapture: Pretribulation, Prewrath, or Posttribulation* (Grand Rapids, MI: Zondervan, 2018), 130.

7. Renald Showers, *The Pre-Wrath View: An Examination and Critique* (Grand Rapids, MI: Kregel, 2001), 33.

The Seal and Trumpet Judgments
Are Warning Signs, Not Divine Wrath

Repent before the great and terrible Day of the Lord!
Prewrath defenders posit that the Day of the Lord begins
with the sixth seal in Revelation 6. They argue that everything prior to this is "birth pangs" (Matthew 24:8) or warning that the Day of the Lord is coming. That said, they do
not typically suggest that the seal and trumpet judgments
are devoid of wrath per se. Instead, it argues that it is devoid
of *God's* wrath. Satanic and/or human wrath is still very
much at play here.

The Rapture Happens Between
the Sixth and Seventh Seals

This is the traditional prewrath view. The church is raptured between seal six and seven and corresponds to the
"great multitude" that comes out of the "great tribulation"
in Revelation 7.[8] Basically, the sixth seal is a preparatory seal
for the wrath of God and the rapture happens in Revelation
7. This is the common view; however, there is another,
more nuanced, view of the prewrath position here and that
is that the rapture happens *before* the sixth seal which deals
with the problem of the traditional view, but comes with

---

8. Showers, *The Pre-Wrath View*, 33.

its own problems.

Chapter Four

Counterarguments to the Prewrath and Posttribulation Views

M UCH OF THE CONTEMPORARY debate surrounding the timing of the rapture hinges not simply
on abstract chronology, but on a theological redefinition
of wrath. Both the prewrath and posttribulation positions
attempt to distinguish between various stages of judgment
in Revelation, proposing that some aspects, particularly the
seal and trumpet judgments, are not expressions of God's
wrath but of Satan's or merely natural consequences. This
chapter engages those claims directly, not to score rhetor-
ical points, but to evaluate whether such distinctions hold
up when measured against the full testimony of Scripture.
While charitable to opposing views, the following analysis
will show that their central assumptions fail to align with
the textual evidence and ultimately diminish the severity
and scope of divine judgment as portrayed in the Apoca-
lypse.

God's Wrath Is Poured on the
Whole Earth, Including the Saints

Matthew 24:21–22 says,

> And there will be great tribulation, such
> as has not been from the beginning of the
> world until now, no, and never will be. And
> if those days had not been cut short, no hu-
> man being would be saved. But for the sake
> of the elect those days will be cut short.

A major challenge in interpreting this passage lies in
Jesus' statement that there has never been, and never will
be, a greater tribulation. If, as some prewrath interpreters
argue, the tribulation ends after the fifth or sixth seal, then
Jesus is simply wrong in his assessment of this tribulation
to come. The judgments that follow, the trumpet and bowl
judgments, are as bad as, if not worse than, the earlier
seals. This suggests that the tribulation does not conclude
midway through Revelation but extends through the latter
judgments as well. While this argument touches on content
addressed in the next section, it supports the conclusion
that the trumpet and bowl judgments should be included
in the tribulation discussion.

That said, the main point for this section is that there
are elect on the earth who would be wiped out if the tribulation of those days were not cut short. The posttribulational view argues that the saints are present during the

tribulation but are somehow exempt from the wrath of God. However, Jesus' words here push back against that idea. He does not say the elect will be preserved through the tribulation; he says the days are shortened because they would not survive otherwise. In other words, Jesus does not describe the elect as divinely shielded from judgment. He describes them as being in real danger—so much so that divine intervention is necessary to prevent their destruction. This is difficult to square with the claim that believers can endure God's wrath untouched. It seems instead that they would be consumed by it unless the period is cut short.

From a posttribulational perspective, this requires a delicate distinction: that believers are not the target of God's wrath, yet would still be destroyed by it if the timeline were not mercifully adjusted. But that distinction raises its own questions. If they are not subject to wrath, why are they threatened by it to the point of needing the days shortened? This does not appear to be a "preservation through wrath" situation. It appears to be a case where the wrath is so severe that the elect would not survive unless God steps in and shortens the timeframe.

Of course, from a pretribulational view, this brings up a different problem. Specifically, how can there be "elect" still on earth if the rapture has already occurred, especially given that, in Matthew 24, the rapture-like event occurs after the "great tribulation," which, if not shortened, would leave no one standing?

I do not intend to answer that question fully in this volume. Suffice to say that the position I will argue for has to do with converts from within the Tribulation. This will be a major focus of the larger work of which this book will be a chapter. For now, it is sufficient to acknowledge that Jesus' words here challenge the assumptions of both major rapture positions, and that any view must take seriously Jesus' plain statement that both the wrath of God and the survival of the elect intersect during this period.

Another example of this tension appears in the contrast between Revelation 2:10 and 3:10–11. In 2:10, it is clear that the tribulation being faced is local and that the faithful are expected to endure it. Revelation 3:10–11, on the other hand, speaks of a coming "hour of trial" that will affect "the whole world," and explicitly promises that those who have kept the word of Jesus will be kept from that hour of trial. The distinction between local tribulation and global wrath is not subtle—it is directly stated in the text.

Additionally, Romans 2:5–8, as noted earlier, directly connects the "day of wrath" with the term "tribulation" in verse 8. This is important because one of the main claims of the prewrath position is that the tribulation is distinct from the day of the Lord. Yet Paul links them explicitly. The "day of wrath" is not something separate from tribulation; it is the context in which tribulation is poured out on those who reject the truth and follow unrighteousness.

The Seal and Trumpet Judgments Can Best Be Understood as Divine Wrath

One must ask the question of whether it really *is* significant that *wrath* is not used for the first five seals, as Rosenthal suggests. Before engaging directly with this question, it is best to note that there are many instances in Scripture where something is talked about without using a specific word. Renald E. Showers writes,

> The presence of a word in the Bible is not the only factor that determines whether it is right or wrong to use that word within a certain biblical concept. If the concept being represented by that word is related to a biblical context, then it is right to use that word for that context even when the word itself is not in the biblical text."[1]

Though he is specifically discussing *tribulation*, this concept also applies to *wrath*. He goes on to, quite thoroughly, demonstrate that *tribulation* is a valid word to describe the "birth pangs" of the first half of the Tribulation. An interesting thing to note here is that 1 Thessalonians 5:3 has the *Day of the Lord* as being the "labor pains." This is the same word that the prewrath position argues for regarding the Tribulation of Matthew 24 and Revelation 6 as being somehow different from the Tribulation of the Day of the Lord. The birth pangs are not considered to be part of the Tribulation as the position argues that

---

1. Showers, *The Pre-Wrath Rapture View*, 12.

the Tribulation starts at the Abomination of Desolation halfway through the seventieth week of Daniel.[2]

The idea that the seal and trumpet judgments are warning signs of God's rather than God's wrath itself is a challenge that must be addressed. If the seal and trumpet judgments involve God's divine wrath, then both prewrath and midtribulation views ought to be rejected. That is precisely what will be argued here. However, there is one potential counterargument that will be addressed in the next section.

The first thing to be noted is that each of the seven seals happens directly due to the action of God himself. An example of this would be Revelation 6:1. Paul Feinberg writes, "The activity of the whole period proceeds from the activity of the worthy Lamb; it is He who breaks the seals."[3] Everything to do with the seals requires the Lamb to initiate it. This is problematic for the view that it is only the wrath of humans and Satan early on in the seals. To be sure, this wrath *is* likely in view here as well. Rather than divorcing the human and/or satanic actions from the direct intervention of God, it is best to realize that God is *using* them, at least partially, to accomplish his will. This is commonly seen in the Old Testament when God would turn his wrath on his own people due to their unbelief. Other nations would come to destroy them and take many

---

2. Rosenthal, *The Pre-Wrath Rapture of the Church*, 161.

3. Paul D. Feinberg, *The Rapture: Pre-, Mid-, or Post-Tribulational?* (Grand Rapids, MI: Zondervan, 1984), 62.

captive and it is taught that this is God's doing. Therefore, any wrath in the first five seals is an outpouring of God's wrath. *However*, this leads to the next point.

Few, if any, of the seal signs can rightly be attributed to the humans, Satan, or the Antichrist. Consider, for example, the fourth seal which is the fourth horseman. Revelation 6:8 says,

> And I looked, and behold, a pale horse! And its rider's name was Death, and Hades followed him. And they were given authority over a fourth of the earth, to kill with sword and with famine and with pestilence and by wild beasts of the earth.

This rider's name is Death and Hades followed him and they killed with the sword, famine, pestilence, and wild beasts. Technically, these things could be attributed to Satan or maybe the post-death Antichrist, but it is more easily understood as being from God through an angel of some sort. Additionally, the fifth seal seems to occur completely in heaven which is outside of the influence of any of these three.

Another problem is that the sixth seal, after which the rapture happens according to the prewrath view, specifically references God's wrath. A plain reading of this section of Revelation demonstrates that this multitude (which according to the prewrath view is the raptured church) would have experienced God's wrath. The only way for the prewrath position to avoid this is to suggest that the rapture happened prior to the sixth seal being opened somehow. However, there is no textual evidence to support this, and I have found only one scholar arguing for this position and he has argued that he is *not* a traditional prewrath rapturist. He does argue mostly along the lines of the prewrath view but also disagrees with it on some points. This author, Samuel Gray Ramsey, states,

> They [the signs of Matthew 24 and seals of Revelation 6] cover the whole tribulation period. Christians face every moment of the signs and seals. Christians are raptured from earth before the day of the Lord begins in Revelation 6:17. This is the moment God begins to pour out His wrath on earth.[4]

There are a couple of things wrong with this. First off, he contradicts himself. If the seals "cover the whole tribulation period" and Christians "face every moment of the signs and seals" then the rapture cannot happen until *after* the seventh seal in Revelation 8:1 or even after the seventh trumpet in Revelation 11. This latter option would be based on the fact that the seventh seal *contains* the seven trumpets. Also, interestingly, on page 164 of the same dissertation, he states that the rapture passage of Revelation is

---

4. Ramsey, "The Day of the Lord Separates Tribulation from Wrath," 17.

7:9–17 and that it is the *only* rapture passage in Revelation. This begs the question: How does that work with the statement that the rapture happens before Revelation 6:17? Yet, he argues that the rapture happens *before* the sixth seal (it has to if the church is not destined for wrath). The second issue is that he provides no evidence from Revelation 6 itself that would point to the rapture at this point. Overall, it makes much better sense to view the "great multitude" as the martyrs who are coming out of the Tribulation as this *does* have textual evidence. The fifth seal (Revelation 6:9–11) demonstrates this quite well.

Potential Difference in the Wrath Poured Out in the Seven Bowls

Now we get to the counterargument alluded to earlier. The seven bowls have the *potential* to be different than the previous references to God's wrath. This whole argument is based on the specific usage of the term "seven bowls of the wrath of God" (Revelation 16:1). These bowls are *specifically* said to contain God's wrath. Thus, it is possible that the bowls are the wrath of God that 1 Thessalonians states believers will not be part of and that everything up to this point was a prelude of some sort. This is essentially a nuanced prewrath view rather than a nuanced midtribulation view that many prewrath views are. Thus, there is a *possibility* that God's wrath is truly poured out during the seven bowls of God's wrath. Additionally, referring to the loud voice from the temple that commanded the angels to pour out their bowls, Leon Morris says, "John is telling us that the plagues are released by none less than God."[5] Other commentators agree that this is likely God himself speaking.[6] That said, there are problems with this whole idea. To begin with, Revelation 15:1 states, "Then I saw another sign in heaven, great and amazing, seven angels with seven plagues, which are the last, for with them *the wrath of God is finished*" (emphasis added).[7] The best way to understand this is to say that the bowls of God's wrath are the last *part* of God's wrath rather than God's "true" wrath. Furthermore, in view of the previous section on the seals and trumpets, it makes the most sense to treat the whole of those as part of God's outpouring of wrath on the earth. These likely cannot be separated from the seven bowls. Therefore, though there is a *possibility* of a later outpouring of God's wrath in the seven bowls, it is not a *likely* interpretation.

Overall, the position advocated in this work is best described as a modified pretribulational view—a view that affirms the rapture occurs prior to the onset of the Tribulation but holds this position with enough theological humility to allow for a slight adjustment if certain scriptural

---

5. Leon Morris, *Revelation: An Introduction and Commentary* (Downers Grove, IL: InterVarsity Press, 1987), 185.

6. See, for example, G. K. Beale, *The Book of Revelation: A Commentary on the Greek Text* (Grand Rapids, MI: Eerdmans, 2013), 770-71.

7. Leon Morris, *Revelation: An Introduction and Commentary* (Downers Grove, IL: InterVarsity Press, 1987), 185.

nuances warrant it. Unlike traditional pretribulationalism, which often treats the timing of the rapture as a settled dogma and potentially over-emphasizes the unity of the judgments, this modified view recognizes that while the pretribulational model fits the biblical evidence best, there remains a nonzero possibility that a more nuanced form of the prewrath position is also technically possible. The defining mark of this view, then, is its exegetical conviction without eschatological arrogance, seeking faithfulness over finality in matters where the text allows for reasonable caution.

CHAPTER FIVE

THE VALUE OF ACKNOWLEDGING THE POSSIBILITY OF A LATER OUTPOURING OF WRATH

F ROM WHAT CAN BE seen above, it is more reasonable to hold to the view that *all* of the Tribulation involves God's wrath, which would necessitate a pretribulation view; however, there is a *possibility* of a later outpouring of divine wrath. Even if there is only a one percent or lower chance of this being true it is worthwhile to note it as it helps one deal with some of the problems often associated with a pretribulation view.

Dealing with the Escapism Mentality

Pretribulationists often run into the problem of having an escapism mentality. This is typically due to a bad understanding of suffering and tribulation in the life of a Christian, but it is there, nonetheless. After all, "all the views also agree that the protection from divine wrath during the Day of the Lord does not mean that the church is exempt from all suffering, trials, persecution, and troubl e."[1] While this may be true of scholars and theologians, it does not necessarily translate to the more general believers. This escapist mentality is actually one of the most used arguments against the pretribulation rapture. For example, David Currie gives a bunch of real-life examples of this problem and the next one as a reason to reject this rapture view. He writes of an elderly woman missionary to China who was extremely sorrowful for teaching that the rapture would take believers before the Tribulation.[2] Unfortunately, when tribulation came to China, her people were woefully unprepared. While the ultimate way to solve this problem is to teach the "whole counsel of God" (Acts 20:27) by having a robust theology of Christian suffering, the knowledge that God's wrath, and thus the rapture, *could* come later in the Tribulation can help combat this difficulty with the pretribulation view. I am, for example, quite certain that God's wrath begins with the first of the seals being opened; however, I hold this loosely enough to allow for being wrong as both a means of fighting against the escapist mentality and avoiding the real danger of the next section.

---

1. Mark Hitchcock, *Can We Still Believe in the Rapture?* (Eugene, OR: Harvest House Publishers, 2017), 139.

2. David Currie, *Rapture: The End-Times Error that Leaves the Bible Behind* (Manchester, NH: Sophia Institute Press, 2003), xviii.

Avoiding Damaged Faith

What happens if the Tribulation starts, and the rapture has not happened? How shaken will the faith of those who are hardcore pretribulationists be? Enough to reject God? One would hope that recognizing the Tribulation as a fulfillment of Scripture would prevent this, but that is not guaranteed by any means. Currie, once again, gives many examples of this. One of which appears to be a personal story. He tells of a young boy who, upon arriving home, found it empty. Having been raised in a home that taught the pretribulation rapture, his first thoughts were that he had been left behind. This caused a crisis of faith within him.[3] It is possible that this whole situation could have been avoided had the boy's family given some level of allowance for being wrong about the pretribulation rapture. It is better to recognize that one might be wrong on the rapture, even if it is by a long shot, than risk losing one's faith or harming the faith of another believer.

---

3. Currie, *Rapture*, xviii.

CHAPTER SIX

SO WHAT?

O NE'S VIEW OF REVELATION, the rapture, and the nature of God's wrath is not just an academic exercise. These are not distant speculations about a far-off future. They are truths that shape how we live, what we value, and how urgently we act. A right understanding of God's wrath in Revelation should lead to a right ordering of one's life under God's authority and mercy.

If the Tribulation is indeed an expression of God's wrath, not merely a chaotic series of events or Satanic onslaughts, then we must treat it with the weight it demands. The end of the age is not merely the unfolding of history, it is God acting in holy judgment against a world that has rejected his Son, the Lamb. That reality should unsettle the complacent, embolden the faithful, and mobilize the church.

Knowing that divine wrath is not just coming eventually, but is unleashed at the opening of the seals, should light a fire under the believer. It means judgment begins sooner than many expect. It means the call to repentance is more urgent than ever. And it means that evangelism is not optional. If people are marching toward a judgment they do not see, and if that judgment is closer than they think, how could we stay silent?

But it is not only about others. If God's wrath falls upon all unrighteousness, how can we, who claim the name of Christ, walk in compromise or indifference? This vision of wrath should stir us to pursue holiness, to repent of every hidden sin, and to walk the narrow path with our eyes fixed on Jesus. The church must not sleep while the world burns.

So then, urgently seek the lost. Speak the truth in love. Pray for mercy. Live as though eternity is near—because it is. And resolutely stand with God, knowing that Jesus has promised he was returning soon. "Behold, I am coming soon, bringing my recompense with me, to repay each one for what he has done" (Revelation 22:12).

Amen. Come, Lord Jesus.

CHAPTER SEVEN

CONCLUSION

O NE OF THE MOST important—and often over-looked—questions in discussions surrounding the rapture is this: What actually constitutes God's wrath in Revelation? The answer to that question carries immense theological and practical significance. It is not a peripheral matter, it is central to our understanding of God's activity in the end times, our placement of the rapture, and how we prepare ourselves and others for what lies ahead.

This book has argued that, based on a careful reading of Revelation's text, the entire Tribulation period is an expression of divine wrath. From the moment the first seal is broken, what unfolds is not merely chaos, not merely satanic deception, and not merely human wickedness, it is the righteous judgment of God against a world that has rejected the Lamb. The cumulative testimony of Revelation, including its explicit references to wrath (such as in Revelation 6, 14, 15, and 16), compels us to see the Tribulation as God's wrath in full motion from beginning to end.

This conclusion has critical implications. It challenges

the foundations of both the midtribulational and prewrath positions, which depend on a later starting point for God's judgment. If those positions are wrong on the nature and timing of divine wrath, then their entire rapture timing frameworks are called into question.

That said, we must maintain theological humility. While the pretribulational position appears to be the most biblically consistent, it is not without its difficulties. A nuanced form of the prewrath view, one that recognizes the early stages of judgment as containing divine purpose, but holds to a distinction in intensity or scope, may offer some merit. Thus, it is wise to hold the pretribulational view with conviction, but not with arrogance. We should be firm in our belief, but flexible enough to account for the possibility, however small the possibility might be, of interpretive error. This guards us from the kind of dogmatism that weakens the church's witness and from the theological tunnel vision that leads to unnecessary division. It also helps deal with the challenge that, though God has revealed much about the end, it is yet a *future* event. In such cases, it is best to hold firmly to one's biblical convictions but allow room in those convictions to be wrong. The key is making sure that we are letting Scripture guide us rather than trying to force a certain view on Scripture.

In the end, this issue is not about winning an eschatological debate. It is about rightly handling the Word of truth. It is about preparing the church to endure, to witness, and to hope. For whether wrath begins in chapter six or later, the Lamb is returning, and he is bringing recompense with him. Our task is not to predict dates or settle every timeline, but to remain faithful, sober-minded, and watchful. The wrath of God is real. The call of the gospel is urgent. And the return of Christ is certain.

A BRIEF CALL TO ACTION

If you found value in this book, please consider leaving an honest review on your favorite book review site (Amazon, BookBub, Goodreads, etc.). Reviews are tremendously helpful to authors. They are, in many ways, the lifeblood of a book and I highly appreciate each one that I receive.

Also, if you are interested in receiving updates on books, book reviews, and other short teachings that I publish, you can follow me on:

- Facebook (Meta): L. J. Anderson at www.facebook.com/profile.php?id=61553506423559

- YouTube: L. J. Anderson at www.youtube.com/@ljandersonbooks

- My website: www.ljandersonbooks.com

ALSO BY L. J. ANDERSON

Books

- *Contending for the Truth: A Biblical Look at Thirteen Contentious Doctrines*

Short Books

- *Theology and Apologetics: An Examination of How and Where They Intersect*

- *The Moral Argument: Is It Worth Having in Your Apologetic Repertoire?*

- *The Inerrancy of Scripture: An Overview and Defense*

- *Hebrews 6:1–8: An Exegetical Strike Against Eternal Security* (coming soon!)

- *Gnosticism: A Biblical and Historical Response* (coming soon!)

BIBLIOGRAPHY

Beale, G. K. *The Book of Revelation: A Commentary on the Greek Text*. Grand Rapids, MI: Eerdmans, 2013.

Currie, David. *Rapture: The End-Times Error that Leaves the Bible Behind*. Manchester, NH: Sophia Institute Press, 2003.

Ehrman, Bart D. *Armageddon: What the Bible Really Says About the End*. New York: Simon & Schuster, 2023.

Erikson, Millard. *Christian Theology*. Grand Rapids, MI: Baker Academic, 2013.

Feinberg, Paul D. *The Rapture: Pre-, Mid-, or Post-Tribulational?* Grand Rapids, MI: Zondervan, 1984.

Harrison, Norman B. *The End: Re-Thinking the Revelation*. Minneapolis, MN: The Harrison Service, 1948.

Hitchcock, Mark. *Can We Still Believe in the Rapture?* Eugene, OR: Harvest House Publishers, 2017.

Hultberg, Alan, ed. *Three Views on the Rapture: Pretribulation, Prewrath, or Posttribulation*. Grand Rapids, MI: Zondervan, 2018.

Morris, Leon. *Revelation: An Introduction and Commentary*. Downers Grove, IL: InterVarsity Press, 1987.

Osborne, Grant. *Revelation*. Grand Rapids, IL: Baker Publishing, 2002.

Showers, Renald E. *The Pre-Wrath Rapture View: An Examination and Critique*. Grand Rapids, MI: Kregel, 2001.

Ramsey, Samuel Gray. "The Day of the Lord Separates Tribulation from Wrath" (2023). Doctoral Dissertations and Projects. 4760.

Rosenthal, Marvin J. *The Pre-Wrath Rapture of the Church*. Nashville, TN: Thomas Nelson, 1990.

Ryrie, Charles C. *Revelation*. Chicago, IL: Moody Publishers, 2018.

Zuck, Roy B., ed. *Vital Prophetic Issues: Examining Promises and Problems in Eschatology*. Grand Rapids, MI: Kregel Resources, 1995.

ABOUT THE AUTHOR

L. J. Anderson is an independent scholar, author, and founder of **Lamad Press**, an academic imprint dedicated to publishing biblically grounded theological works. He holds a Master of Divinity and is currently pursuing a PhD in theology, where his dissertation research focuses on developing a new model of God. This model seeks to offer a coherent and biblically faithful framework capable of addressing longstanding challenges to the doctrine of God—particularly those related to the Trinity.

This work represents a piece of that broader research agenda, contributing to the reevaluation of traditional theological formulations in light of Scripture. Anderson aims to bridge the gap between philosophical coherence and scriptural fidelity, crafting theological models that remain both rigorous and accessible.

He has published several books through Lamad Press, including *The Inerrancy of Scripture* and *The Moral Argument*, and his writings are indexed in Google Scholar. As a disabled veteran, he is able to devote his time to research, writing, and publishing, with the long-term goal of establishing Lamad Press as a trusted source for independent academic theology.

He is also the founder of **Lamad Christian Books**, a curated online bookstore offering academic and devotional Christian works, Christian fiction, and clean non-Christian fiction. You can learn more at **ljandersonbooks.com** and **lamadpress.com**.

www.ingramcontent.com/pod-product-compliance
Lightning Source LLC
Chambersburg PA
CBHW051336120626
46547CB00016B/2567